Do You Hear What I Hear?

How to Start Your Christmas Caroling Business in 7 Steps

by

Susan P. Sloan and Randy J. Pope

Disclaimer

This book has been written for information purposes only. Every effort has been made to make this book as complete and accurate as possible; however, there may be mistakes in typography or content that went unnoticed during review. Information contained herein may be outdated after publication; therefore, this book should be used only as a guide and not the ultimate source.

The purpose of this book is to educate readers. The author and publisher do not warrant that the information given here is fully complete and shall not be responsible for any errors or omissions. The author and publisher shall have neither liability nor responsibility to any person or entity with respect to any loss or damage caused or alleged to be caused directly or indirectly by this book.

Table of Contents

Foreword

For as long as I can remember, I've been involved in music: piano lessons, school choirs, church choirs (both participant and teacher/director), school band, various community and civic music groups, and owner of a music talent management studio. Each has had its own purpose, learning curve, audience, and value. However, in this span - over half a century - no experience has been more rewarding or heartwarming than being a part of The Queen's Carolers, the group that Susan and Randy formed.

Some of the best, most memorable experiences in my five years with the group include the receptive and attentive audience of Teen Challenge (my very favorite place to sing). Another precious moment occurred when we allowed a retired choir director to conduct our group on her favorite song, "God Rest Ye Merry, Gentlemen." This was during her family's Christmas vacation; we learned later that she died just after Christmas.

Good audience participation for "The Twelve Days of Christmas" can make us lose our focus, making it even funnier. At almost every venue, having children (and sometimes adults) participate with "Jingle Bells" can make our day, as do the heartfelt thanks we get from listeners everywhere.

The last line of "Good King Wenceslas" sums it up best: "Ye who now will bless the poor shall yourselves find blessing."

Go find your blessings.

Susan Bailey
Forté Studio

Preface: What We Heard

We first joined a caroling group as part of a church outreach ministry back in 1999. Other members of our family participated for a while, but the two of us (brother and sister) were "hooked" from the start.

This probably was because we grew up in a singing family. For years our lives often included weekend trips to various churches across Georgia, Alabama, and north Florida, singing with our parents.

We also have a strong heritage of memorizing and reciting verse, both secular and sacred. As young people who grew up in church, we frequently participated in plays and skits, so public speaking came naturally to us as well.

In short, everything about the caroling group just fit with our background. We heard the call and followed.

Several changes in our lives and in the focus of that ministry opened the way for us to start our own caroling ensemble. Rather than competing with our former group, we chose to operate as a business, a situation that benefitted both groups.

After some preliminary research and canvassing for singers, we officially "opened for business" in late 2005. Other details are provided within this little manual, which we hope will assist you in your caroling business endeavors.

Introduction: What You Might Hear

In our case, this was a seasonal activity that we wanted to continue, but we no longer had a solid church choir to provide us with singers. We also wanted to offer our services to an entirely different set of clients, some of whom might express reluctance at using a group associated with a local church. Here are other reasons to consider:

Setting up as a business opens new doors. Some professional people seem to be more comfortable engaging other businesses for their events, and there might be venues that would be considered inappropriate for a church group. Whether to work in such venues is totally up to the owner and performers in a business situation.

As a business, you can charge a fee for your performances to offset your expenses. Without the backing of a strong church, all expenses fall to the group promoter. Additionally, you have to pay your singers. Setting up as business allows you to do that.

You can control membership in your group. Churches rely heavily on volunteers to carry out their ministries. As a business, you have the power to employ the people you want.

The commitment is limited by the seasonal aspect of the group. Probably everyone in your group will be bound to a regular job or other daily activities, so the limited time frame of caroling allows them to earn extra money without a long-term commitment.

One business can serve other purposes. If you have other projects or services to offer, such as providing music lessons, you can group everything under one business umbrella. Once you have everything set up, the caroling portion should take little of your time.

The monetary investment is small. Whether you decide to buy, rent, or make your own costumes, the capital invested for this type of business is small compared to others. If you have contacts who own a bridal/formal shop, a fabric outlet or second-hand store, you may be able to work out an arrangement with them. You can also explore the drama departments of nearby colleges or high schools for costume loans, advice, or assistance. Most items can be purchased on the Internet as well, so you don't have to spend valuable time shopping all over town for the right items.

The wonder of the season still appeals; the message is the same. As carolers, you invite the audience to step away from their present-day cares and to reminisce about childhood, family closeness, the joy of giving or receiving gifts, and holiday memories. In this somewhat-scripted atmosphere, people often feel free to shed a tear, share a smile, and open their hearts to the joy and hope of the season.

Perhaps that's because the carols remind us that we all belong to a struggling, hurting humanity, unworthy of the great gift of Love that God bestowed on us. And yet He gave Christ to us and for us, in spite of ourselves.

That's the wonder of Christmas. That's why we sing.

Step 1: Calling Others

To be sure that you have a product to offer in your business, you will need singers. You may already have a few people in mind, but you must realize that they have to meet a few requirements.

Singer Requirements

You may want to add other requirements to this list. The basic requirements are as follows:

- sing a cappella (unless you plan to have a mobile instrument for accompaniment)
- blend with other voices and hold their part

- commit to attending a certain number of regular rehearsals and the performance schedule
- provide their own costume (unless you make other arrangements)
- stand or stroll for an hour or more while singing

Most people don't realize how taxing it can be to sing for an hour, and you may have performances that go longer.

Finding Singers

If you don't have a set of singers readily available, here are some suggestions for finding more:

- Contact the music ministers at various local churches
- Ask voice teachers or directors at local colleges or universities

- Check with local high school chorus directors
- Put a notice on Meet-up or a community bulletin board*
- Post a notice on social media*

*Do this at your own discretion; you may get replies that are not what you want.

Probably the **best** way to find singers is to announce auditions. You may put such an announcement in church bulletins and give it verbally during rehearsals for the vocal groups noted above. Here's a sample announcement you might try:

Attention singers! Come and audition for a select group of paid performers for the Christmas season. Auditions will be held at (place) on (date) from/to (times). Call (phone #) to schedule your time.

You can explain all the requirements (listed above) when they show up for the audition. It would be wise to include group singing in your auditions, not just individual performances, to check how well each person's voice blends with others.

Beyond Singing

Conduct auditions for speaking parts, too. Your speakers should know how to project their speaking voices as well as how to add appropriate emphasis, facial expressions, and body language, besides being able to memorize lines and enunciate clearly. If you decide to use a specific accent, as we did, each speaker must be able to adapt a believable accent so that you create a cohesive unit.

Depending on the size of your group, you will need key individuals to help you keep things on track. You can designate a music leader, appointment coordinator, drama coach, or group leader, according to your needs.

The appointment coordinator and drama coach do not have to be carolers, so you can include people who cannot or do not want to sing, if you wish. You may also want to arrange for someone to take photographs or videos. You can use video and pictures to help you pinpoint problems, to add to advertising, and to serve as historical records.

How Many Carolers?

You may have as few as four singers, one on each part—soprano, alto, tenor, and bass (SATB)—or as many as you think you will need. You can start small and add more next year. Our group usually consisted of ten to fourteen adult singers and a couple of children on occasion. This allowed for scheduling two small groups at the same time or for overlapping times and also for a large group when one was requested.

Step 2: Getting Legal

Like any other business in town, you will need to meet the business requirements of your local government. This could include several forms and fees, so check with your city or county courthouse to determine exactly what you need.

Business Legal Requirements

Even before all the local requirements are satisfied, you can register for a tax identification (TID) number if you're in the United States. This is an easy process that is completed online. The most difficult choice probably will be deciding on the type of business you want to set up—whether an LLC, Corporation, Single Proprietor, Partnership, etc.

Your TID sets you up as a credible business and is used when you file your tax information. Some clients will require a form (W9 in the U. S.) with that number so they can use it in their accounting system.

If you are outside the U. S., please check your country's website to see what is needed.

Business Supplies

You probably can use your home address as your business address; just be sure to use the same address in all your documents. Supplies that you will want to keep on hand include: business cards, songbooks or folders for music, flyers to send with your letters or display in prominent locations, postcards, invoices, and some kind of schedule planner for engagements.

You can create most of those things yourself on your computer to save money. For samples or templates, search online by form type, for example, "sample invoice" or "postcard template."

Naming Your Business or Group

One important element to consider is how you will identify your group. We chose to set up our business with a name that could easily encompass other ideas that we wanted to try later. Thus, the caroling group was a product that the business offered. Later, when we decided to retire from the group, we were able to pass on the product to someone else.

No Standard Employees

Because this is a seasonal business, you don't need to have regular employees. Your singers can work on a contract basis. In the U. S., contract workers don't have to include this income in their tax filing as long as it's less than a certain amount (currently $600). This also simplifies your accounting, since you don't have to furnish them with a tax document unless they ask for it.

Forms and Records

That brings us to some forms that you will need for your singers. You can download samples of these from the Internet. We strongly urge you to give these to your singers and get them returned to you, if possible, before your first engagement.

These include liability/hold harmless agreements, photo release forms, audio recording release forms, and contract employee forms. These are to protect you against future legal action.

Be sure to keep good records of all your expenses, including transportation for any venue outside your immediate area. As a small business, you may be required to explain any allowance claimed when you file your taxes. You should open a separate bank account for your business for receiving and distributing funds.

Don't forget to include forms for your clients, such as invoices. You can find a basic form online; just make the necessary changes to adapt it to your needs.

How to Determine Your Fees

Since our rates were based on the number of singers and the length of the program requested, most of our clients asked for the lower numbers (four to six). We looked at the rates charged by similar groups across the country and started with a much lower figure.

After several seasons of complicated record keeping, we learned to start our rates at four singers for one hour, then add a set amount (such as $25 or $30) for *each* singer per *each* half hour.

We always tried to give more value, as well as to plan for sudden illness or other situations, by scheduling extra singers at times. For instance, we would send an extra soprano or someone who was able to carry different parts, so we had five singers instead of the four requested. Naturally, your base rate would have to be set to allow for paying that additional person.

Discounts and Freebies

We felt inclined to give a discount to non-profit groups, so we had to adjust for that in our fees as well. This does complicate your calculations a bit, but we found that it fostered good relationships in the community.

Because everyone in our group came from a church background, they were always willing to include a couple of pro bono performances, too. One of those quickly topped the list of our favorite places to sing each season.

Step 3: Hear Ye, Hear Ye!

A business cannot be successful without clients, of course, and your first year will be the most difficult in that aspect. Once you have proved your worth, many clients will have you back year after year.

Where to Find Clients

Compile a list of businesses that might be looking for entertainment during the Christmas season. Begin with those businesses where you have an established relationship, such as your bank, doctor, lawyer, or your favorite store. Ask if they plan to provide a Christmas party or celebration for their employees or customers.

Announce your new business with a letter to the person who schedules such events. Even though email is faster and more commonly used, a letter on paper gets more attention. It serves as an announcement, a commitment, and a resource for the person you contact.

A sample letter is provided below. Anything that is underlined is where you would substitute your information.

Dear <u>Mr. Curtis</u>:

I'm very excited to tell you about a new group that is designed to help you with your Christmas event this year.

Our group is called <u>Queen Victoria's Carolers</u>, and our purpose is to brighten your holiday event with Christmas caroling during the upcoming holiday season. We can provide a program of 45 - 60 minutes of traditional Christmas songs, as well as a story or two, according to your needs. As our name implies, we will be dressed in our

Victorian costumes and speaking with our best (adopted) British accents.

Please find our list of fees for this service attached. We've kept the rates low so that you can add this delightful entertainment to your event without hurting your bottom line.

This group will be available from November 15 until December 15. Since our group is small, we will have to limit the number of performances that we can make and must finalize our calendar by November 1. Please contact us at your earliest convenience at the number or address given.

Thank you,
Susan Sloan

Other Sources

Besides businesses, also check with community clubs or entities with high visibility, such as your Chamber of Commerce. Our local historical society sponsors a tour of notable homes in our city, and many of these houses are located within a few blocks of each other. We have participated in this tour several times because our costumes fit with that historical period. In situations like this, we can stop and sing at each house or on the street while strolling between the homes and shops.

Appearances at these events serve to let people know about your group. We readily admit that it's sometimes difficult to get the crowd to hear your songs in such open-air places, let alone establish a rapport that allows you to "connect" with your listeners. However, you never know how a phrase in a song or a bit of a story may spark someone's interest and lead to other engagements.

Step 4: Creating a Scene

The one element that will grab the attention of your audience right away is your appearance. That's why choirs wear robes or dress uniformly, to present a complete picture. Nothing screams "Look at me!" like a costume.

Dressing in Costume

When you dress in the style of a different era, special attention must be paid to every detail. Be diligent in your research of styles, in locating patterns and fabric, and in adding the finishing touches. For women especially, this can become a year-long shopping expedition—an occupation that can be both frustrating and delightful.

If you use, as we did, the popular Victorian period, be aware that it extended from 1837 to 1901, and styles changed several times during those 64 years. We suggest that you choose either the early, middle, or late part of that period, each roughly a twenty-year span. You can find information about those fashions in the reference department of your local library or on several web sites. We've listed a few resources in the appendix.

The Victorian Costume

Because we are most familiar with the early Victorian period, we've listed the costume essentials for that era. If you choose another era, pay close attention to the same kinds of details as those listed here.

32

Early Victorian dress for men: Long trousers were popular for day wear, just as they are today; the knee-length knickers with hose were considered formal wear. Jackets tended to be longer and were the precursor to our modern tuxedos, so our modern formal wear would be typical of their everyday wear. In winter months, he might add a caped overcoat similar to a Western duster.

In addition, a waistcoat (vest) and a cravat (precursor to the neck-tie) were considered *de rigueur* (required by current fashion). A Victorian man rarely went anywhere without a hat and gloves, and often he carried a cane for safety as much as for effect. Jewelry would have been limited to rings and a stick-pin in his cravat. In winter, he would wear a many-caped overcoat and perhaps a knitted scarf.

The early Victorian woman wore several layers of petticoats under her dress or skirt, which came to the top of her half-boots. Unlike today, a display of ankles was considered risqué, but a hint of cleavage was not. Though short sleeves were acceptable during the warm months, long sleeves would have been worn during the winter, and her bodice would be more modest for day wear.

She also wore gloves and a bonnet or hat anytime she stepped out of the house, carrying her reticule (draw-string purse). A pelisse, a warm shawl, or a hooded cloak would have gone over her outfit for warmth. A lace collar, ribbons, or a fichu (a swatch of lace inserted in the bodice to cover a low décolletage) might have complemented her dress, and she would have worn rings, necklaces, bracelets, earrings, or perhaps a watch pinned to her bodice. Her hat might be decorated with ribbons, flowers, netting, or feathers.

To Make, Borrow or Buy?

If you have connections with someone who owns a formal shop, a fabric store, a costume rental, a specialty boutique, a second-hand store, or something similar, consider asking that person to help you put your costumes together. Even if you don't know these people, you might approach them with your needs and see if they will offer some assistance.

If you choose to have all your costumes made, appeal to the manager of the store for discounts or donations. Starting early is the key here; you don't want to ask people to help when you're short on time! Be quick to give them credit for helping, too, whether it's an official credit in some document, or just taking the carolers by their shop or house for a brief visit on your way to or from another engagement.

Making your own costume can be fun and not at all difficult for an experienced seamstress or tailor. Just match the pattern to your skills. Every year we see more patterns for costumes in the fabric shops. For the early to middle Victorian period, you can adapt fashions from the American Civil War, or even patterns of formal dresses. Try to match styles from *Little Women, Gone with the Wind,* or even *Little House on the Prairie.*

For the late Victorian period, look for references to Gibson girls or *The Music Man.* You can use many modern fabrics that mock the original, such as poplin or gabardine for bombazine, or perhaps velour instead of velvet. Do consider your climate and whether performances will be inside or outside. We recommend light fabrics for our Southern neighbors.

Color Combinations

You may want to consider color combinations now, if you know that certain people (a couple or family with children) will prefer to stay together. See our contact information at the end of this book if you would like to see pictures.

Many people think they should wear traditional Christmas colors—red and green. We would advise caution with that. There are so many shades of red and green, you could have a problem with those clashing. Encourage your people to wear the colors that look best on them; they can always bring in elements of the season with accessories. The men typically wear brown, black, or gray.

Step 5: Rocking & Rolling

Now that your costumes are in process, you need to begin rehearsals. You or your music leader will select and provide music for the songs to be included in your program.

Getting to the Music

Fortunately, getting enough copies of music is easier when you use older Christmas carols because you don't have to secure permission to perform them; they have passed into public domain. If your arrangement is recent, however, be sure that you buy enough copies for everyone or obtain written permission to photocopy it from the publisher.

A competent leader will assure that his group gets the words and music memorized, blends well, and sings to be understood. We offer a word of caution on timing: do not let these songs drag or run away on you, as some have a tendency to do; your audience will notice!

Here's a list of the songs we have included in our program, with some variation from year to year. Others were on our "wish list" to include at a future date. Although several are considered "musts" and are always included, it's fun to mix them up from time to time.

We've included some comments on each song listed. You may also want to purchase our *Scripts and Stories for Christmas Carolers* to provide speaking parts that can be used between songs.

Our Repertoire

Please note: Although we've entitled the book after a popular modern carol, that song is not included in our repertoire. That's because it was written in the Twentieth Century, and we chose to limit our songs to those that would have been sung during the Victorian period.

"Here We Come A-caroling"—This is our introductory song, sometimes performed as we enter the venue. If your music uses the word "wassailing" instead of "caroling," please change it as a way of letting people know that your purpose is to sing.

"Angels from the Realms of Glory" You can probably find this beautiful song in a church hymnal.

"Angels We Have Heard on High"
This song easily can be blended with
"Hark! the Herald Angels Sing" If
you like to flow from one song to another
without a break. Both are included in
most church hymnals.

"Away in a Manger" This is a good
one for the children in your group. You
might want them to do one (or all) of the
verses without adult assistance.

"Coventry Carol" Though it is
hauntingly beautiful, you may find this
song difficult to include because of its
serious nature. Make sure that your
audience understands the story and how
it relates to the Christmas message.

"Deck the Hall" Some of the words,
though familiar to us, aren't easily

understood, so you can explain them in your monologue.

"God Rest Ye Merry, Gentlemen" Here's another song with outdated words; you can find a monologue to introduce this song in our companion booklet, *Scripts and Stories for Christmas Carolers*.

"Good Christian Men, Rejoice" This one is often included in church hymnals.

"Good King Wenceslaus" We divide the men and women on the verses: the men sing the words spoken by Wenceslaus, and the women sing the words of the page. Everyone sings together on the remaining, narrative portions. That helps to support the story embedded in the song.

"I Saw Three Ships" This song has more verses than you'll want to include probably, but it is truly Victorian. We divide the verses between the men and women in a question-and-answer style.

"It Came upon a Midnight Clear" Here's a really beautiful song with many verses from which to choose.

"Jingle Bells" Of American origin, this one is fun and easy to sing for children of all ages. We carry bells with us to bring out for this song; if appropriate, we invite children from the audience to ring the bells for us.

"Joy to the World" Speaking to the very heart of Christmas, this one is great for inviting your audience to sing along.

"Little Children, Can You Tell?"
From the Victorian era, this is a
question-and-answer song, featuring the
children on the two middle verses.

"O Christmas Tree" It's appropriate
to include this song for Victorian carolers
because Queen Victoria's German
husband, Prince Albert, was largely
responsible for reviving Christmas
celebrations in England.

"O Come, All Ye Faithful" Here's
another one from the church hymnal
that everyone will know.

"O Come, Emmanuel" We
recommend having a strong soprano or
tenor for the melody of this lovely song.

"O Little Town of Bethlehem" The
harmony can be difficult, but you could

pare it down to a duet or create a medley with another song to make it easier. It makes for a lovely segue into *Silent Night.*

"Ring, Christmas Bells" This is another version of *Carol of the Bells*; we prefer it because the words focus on Christ.

"Silent Night" This is the number one song that people expect to hear, and it has a rich heritage to tell. We include a solo or duet of the first verse in the original German.

"The First Noel" Full of beautiful, moving parts, this song has several verses from which to choose.

"The Twelve Days of Christmas" We included two monologues to introduce this song in *Scripts and Stories for Christmas Carolers*. This is a great song to use for audience participation by creating motions for each verse and inviting everyone to join you.

"What Child is This?" The mix of minor and major chords make this a hauntingly beautiful song with words that explain the Christmas story.

"(We Wish You) A Merry Christmas" This is always our last song, popular because even young children can sing most of the words.

Using Scripts and Stories

Memorized script--a collection of several short monologues--is used to introduce the group and the songs. We've included some that we have used over the years in our *Scripts and Stories for Christmas Carolers*. If your group visits the same audiences every year, you probably will want to change your scripts after two or three years. For instance, you could use the Caroling History set for a couple of years, then use the Dickens' World set for a year or two, alternating according to your needs. Of course, you can also come up with your own scripts, but it's challenging to find different things to say about the same songs.

Auditions for solos and speaking parts can be done during regular rehearsals or by appointment. The leader or drama coach should pass out a couple of different speaking parts for participants to use, making it clear that these should be memorized by a specific date. (We suggest no later than November 1.)

If you want to include a story as well, those participants must be able to memorize a rather large quantity of lines. Get our *Scripts and Stories for Christmas Carolers* for a selection of monologues and story suggestions.

Remember that your speakers must be good story tellers; they must be able to project their voices, enunciate clearly, and add suitable facial expressions and body language. If you decide to use foreign accents, each speaker must be good enough that your listeners wonder if their accents are genuine.

There are a number of ways you can assist your people in adopting their new accents. We live in the Southeastern United States, where most people have a slow, relaxed speech pattern. For our caroling group, we decided to use British accents--actually it started as a joke, but we decided it was worth a try. That meant that we had to pronounce every consonant and change our vowels to a more "open" sound. We watched movies with British actors and the BBC on television. We learned that word inflection also varies between English speakers: Americans tend to let the voice fall at the end of sentences, but sometimes Brits let the voice rise, as if asking a question, probably to make the listener think about what's being said.

Step 6: Making Time & Money

The fewer people involved, the easier your scheduling will be; however, you will be limited to the number of engagements you can make. Four people can carry this load, depending on everyone's availability, but you may soon see that you need backup people.

Scheduling Carolers

If you have eight people (two quartets), you can schedule more engagements and also have backups for each part in an emergency. The ideal situation would be for the same four people to sing together all the time, but this has rarely worked for us because of other commitments our people have in their lives.

That being the case, we learned to keep a grid of performance assignments so we could see at a glance who was scheduled to be where. Provide each caroler with a copy of the schedule and give updates as necessary. They will need the following information on their schedule:

- Date
- Client/venue/contact information
- Arrival time
- Program length
- Carolers assigned

Charting Expenses

A similar chart is handy for paying your carolers. You can figure each person's wages due by adding another column to the grid. You can also add other columns to keep track of your total receipts and profits.

That grid can include the following items:

- Date
- Client/venue/contact information
- Arrival time
- Program length
- Carolers assigned
- Gross amount (fee charged)
- Amount paid to carolers
- Net amount (profit)

Receiving and Distributing Funds

Your business bank account is the easiest tool to use for handling money. Have your clients pay by check or cash, if possible. You can set up an account with a service like Square, PayPal, or AplePay, to facilitate credit card payments, but you likely will pay a fee for each transaction using that service.

Check with several banks to see if any will assist you with a low-fee or no-fee checking account. Most will also provide you with a debit card to use for your purchases.

We advise you to pay your carolers by check; if possible, issue only one check to each person at or near the end of the season. By that time, you should have accumulated enough funds in your account to cover their wages.

Step 7: Going Onstage

Now that everyone has been taught the basics, it's time to practice, practice...and practice some more.

The Musical Component

For *a cappella* singing, each group leader needs a pitch pipe to give the starting note of each song and a way to set the tempo. This is easy for Victorian caroling because the men would carry a cane, which makes for a nice director's baton. Practicing with a piano is great, but don't grow to depend on it. The group must learn to blend their voices; they must stay on pitch and in tempo together.

If your group includes children, they will usually sing the melody with the sopranos on most songs. One or two of your songs can feature the children, such as "Little Children, Can You Tell?" or "Away in a Manger." If you have arrangements that are particularly difficult, you might have the children "sit out" those songs. (Literally, they can sit on the floor, if needed.)

You can choose whether you want your carolers to memorize their songs or carry a "songbook" with them. We highly recommend memorizing the songs, even if you choose to carry the music. That way, your group can interact with the audience, rather than burying their noses in a book.

On one hand, if you carry the music, you have your program with you and can refer to it in those moments of utter "blackout" that happen on occasion. On the other hand, not carrying a book frees your hands for grasping rails, making motions as you sing, assisting others, etc.

If you decide to carry the music, we recommend you use nothing larger than a regular composition notebook, and to make it as light as possible. If you use public domain music, you can photocopy on the front and back of each page and compile it in a paper folder with brads to hold the pages. If you use a published book, it will probably be smaller, but not necessarily lighter.

The Visual Component

With the donning of costumes, you enter the world of drama. Every singer, every speaker now becomes an actor in your presentation.

The drama coach now takes center stage as your performers adapt characteristics of the period you have chosen. To walk like a Victorian, our carolers had to concentrate on posture, something that is largely ignored by twenty-first century Americans. There could be no slouching! We had to keep our spines straight, shoulders down and back.

Movements, also, had to be slower than usual and very graceful. When greeting each other, men had to bow or tip their hats and women would curtsey or nod their heads. If the audience applauded, we would bow or curtsey. During strolling and upon entering or exiting the performance area, the men had to be prepared to assist the women, especially with stairs. (The proper way to do this is for the man to extend his arm at a 90-degree angle with his muscles braced to accept her weight; the woman uses one hand to gather and lift her skirts away from her foot and places the other hand on top of the man's extended hand for support.)

We like to include children in our group and try to cluster in "families" as if we were on a family excursion. This insures that adults are always nearby to keep the children focused on the performance. Once we even had an old-fashioned pram (baby carriage) for an infant who went with us. In grouping your families, consider each person's height, costume color, and voice part. You wouldn't want all your altos or all your red outfits concentrated in one spot. Also, your speakers or soloists should be positioned so they can step out when it's time for their part, and your group leader needs to be where everyone can see him or her.

Epilogue: Take a Bow

The first performance is always the toughest, so you might consider making it someplace where you feel more comfortable or where the audience is more forgiving. After that, you'll be able to make any adjustments and feel more at ease with your program.

We wish you much success and joy in your caroling business!

Susan P. Sloan and Randy J. Pope

Please note: If you have questions for us or if you would like us to provide an on-site conference to help your caroling group get started, please contact us at: queenscarolers@yahoo.com.

Additional Resources

❖ *The Christmas Carolers' Book in Song and Story* by Torstein O. Kvamme (available on Amazon)

❖ *The Reader's Digest Merry Christmas Songbook* (available on Amazon)

❖ *Scripts and Stories for Christmas Carolers* (available on Amazon)

You can also check your local library for books with songs or the history of songs or for a collection of short stories about Christmas. Remember that your library has more than books. You can rent movies or videos to study the dialect and behavior that you want to present. The library also may keep a list of organizations in your area that may be of assistance, such as historical societies.

Try your local small business association for any help you need with regulations for your city, state or the federal government. If you use a Certified Public Accountant (CPA), that person could be of tremendous value to you; otherwise, it's up to you to navigate those waters.

Of course, the Internet is a wonderful resource, right at your fingertips. All you do is type in the key word—for instance, Victorian, costume, tuxedo, Christmas carols, etc.—and you'll find a whole world of people waiting to help you.

Sometimes you may have to follow a chain of links to get what you want, but it's there...somewhere. Here are some that we found in our search.

Amazon.com

e-Bay.com

costumepage.org

victorianstations.com

victoriana.com

victorianbazaar.com

victorianweb.org

victorianchoice.com

www.ingramcontent.com/pod-product-compliance
Lightning Source LLC
Chambersburg PA
CBHW071235220526
45468CB00002B/868